Old Orkney
Guthrie Hutton

The north isles have been served by a number of ships, three of which have been named *Orcadia*. The third vessel to bear the name was built at Hall Russell's shipyard in Aberdeen and is seen here shortly after coming into service in 1962. She remained in operation until 1990.

ISBN 9781840334678

GEORGE RENDALL & CO.
1 Albert Street, KIRKWALL,
ORKNEY, Near "SCAPA FLOW."

Shetland Goods.

White Lace Motor Scarfs.
White Lace Handkerchiefs and Shawls.
White Crape Handkerchiefs and Shawls.
Natural Coloured Lace Handkerchiefs and Shawls. In Greys, Fawns, Moorit, Shela, Browns, &c.
Lace Mits, Caps, Ties, Veils & Motor Scarfs. In Black, White, and Natural Colours.
Warm Hap Shawls. In Self, White, Black, and Natural Colours, and with Blended Borders.

Underclothing, &c.

Ladies' White and Grey Combinations. Short and Long Sleeves.
Ladies' White and Grey Vests. Short and Long Sleeves.
Ladies' Spencers, P. Coats, Drawers, Hose, &c.
Gent.'s Vests, Pants, Jerseys, Cardigans, Cravats, Socks, Hose, Lumbago Belts, Knee Caps, &c.
Children's Vests, Combinations, Spencers, P. Coats, Hose, &c.
Ladies', Gent.'s, and Children's Gloves and Mits. In Black, White, Grey, Brown, Moorit, Stripe, Loop, and Checks, &c.

Fair Isle Fancy Hosiery.

Cravats, Jerseys, Night Caps, Smoking and Tam o' Shanter Caps, Socks, Stockings, Gloves, &c.

Orkney Hosiery.

Plain, Ribbed, and Fancy Socks; Golf, Tennis, and Cycling Hose, &c.

George Rendall did business for many years from this imposing shop building, erected opposite Parliament Close in 1904. As the advertisement shows he sold a wide variety of clothing items.

Acknowledgements

With the naivety of youth I once asked the custodian at one of Orkney's ancient monuments (I will not mention which one, to protect the guilty) if Orcadians felt more like Scandinavians or Scots. His answer, that they felt like Orcadians, not only put me firmly in my place, but sparked a sense of admiration and respect for the islands and people that has never left me, although the flower of youth faded long ago. It has thus been a delight to compile this collection of pictures and stories. A number of people have helped in the process and I would consequently like to thank Eric Eunson, Ronnie Rusack, Mark I'Anson, Stuart Marshall, Margeorie Mekie and Gareth Burgess for their assistance. The Orkney Library and Archive was a treasure trove and I am grateful to Stromness Museum for permission to use the pictures of William Hourston on pages 49 (upper), 57 (lower) and 58 (lower). The Royal Naval Museum also helped with some useful pointers, but perhaps the most valuable source of information was the many people who stopped to offer help as I combed the streets and countryside looking for elusive clues. I am grateful to them all.

Further Reading

Allardyce, Keith and Hood, Evelyn M, *At Scotland's Edge*, 1986.

Bathurst, Bella, *The Lighthouse Stevensons*, 1999.

Burgher, Leslie, *Orkney: An Illustrated Architectural Guide*, 1991.

Cormack, Alastair and Anne, *Days of Orkney Steam*, 1971.

Gifford, John, *The Buildings of Scotland: Highlands and Islands*, 1992.

Fenton, Alexander, The Northern Isles, 1978

Ferguson, David M, *Shipwrecks of Orkney, Shetland and Pentland Firth*, 1988.

Hudson, Norman, *Souvenir Post Cards from Orkney*, 1994.

Robertson, John D. M., The Selected Works of Ernest Walker Marwick, *An Orkney Anthology*, Vol. 1, 1991.

Ritchie, Anna, *Exploring Scotland's Heritage, Orkney and Shetland*, revised edition 1993.

Shearer, J, Groundwater, W, and Mackay, J. D. *The New Orkney Book*, 1966.

Tait, Charles, *The Orkney Guide Book*, 1991.

Tinch, David M. N., *Shoal and Sheaf*, 1988.

Van der vat, Dan, *The Grand Scuttle*, 1994.

Introduction

Orkney must have seemed like an earthly paradise to prehistoric people who have left behind enough evidence to suggest that thousands of years ago they populated the islands more heavily than many other parts of Britain or northern Europe. The reasons for this can only be guessed at; the absence of wild animals or wild neighbours perhaps, but the archaeological record is extraordinarily rich and is still being added to with new discoveries.

Some of the most intriguing of the ancient structures are the numerous brochs scattered around the islands. These massive towers appear to have been erected to defend their occupants from a feared aggressor, and because most brochs were built on or near the coast, the danger must have come from the sea. The chief suspects are the Vikings who arrived as hostile hordes, then settled on the islands and used them as a base from which to raid other parts of the British Isles.

When they arrived, the Norsemen discovered that Celtic monks had already brought Christianity to the islands and they too eventually adopted the religion. To celebrate their faith, they built a number of small churches and the magnificent St Magnus Cathedral, and thereafter the church played a prominent role in island affairs.

By the thirteenth century Norway's hold on its distant territories was getting weaker. Orkney and Shetland were ruled by earls, answerable to the Kings of Norway, but the earldom had been held by Scots even before King Hakon was defeated at the Battle of Largs in 1263. Following this setback he returned to Orkney where he died and, after a brief internment in the cathedral, his body was taken back to Norway. That country's influence in Scandinavia was also waning, a process that gained momentum when, under the Kalmar Union, the thrones of Norway, Sweden and Denmark were unified in 1397. Orkney and Shetland were now beholden to a Danish monarch and when his daughter was betrothed to King James III, they were transferred to Scotland as part of her dowry: Orkney in 1468, Shetland the following year.

Scots moved across the Pentland Firth in growing numbers, but when Mary, Queen of Scots granted the earldom to her half brother, Robert Stewart, in 1564, Orcadians discovered the full downside to Scottish rule. The old Udal laws and social structures were swept away as Robert and his son Patrick presided over a brutal feudal regime. Their tyranny ended after fifty years, but lasting damage had been done. The seventeenth century, a time of poverty punctuated by a brief, but relatively positive spell of Cromwellian rule, was followed by the signing of the Act of Union in 1707 which one islander hailed as the best thing Scotland had done for Orkney. Again nothing changed quickly, there was some attempt to reform land use, but increasingly Orcadians turned to the sea, sometimes willingly on whaling ships or trading vessels of the Hudson's Bay Company, sometimes unwillingly as pressed men for the Royal Navy. After the Napoleonic wars, agricultural reform gathered pace and although there were winners and losers Orkney handled the change better than most. There were some brutal 'clearances', notably on Rousay and Wyre, but generally farming practices were transformed so successfully that the foundation was laid for prosperity to grow in the twentieth century.

During the first half of that century Orkney twice found itself at the centre of international affairs when wars prompted the Royal Navy to base its Grand Fleet at Scapa Flow. Two events, the scuttling of the German High Seas Fleet in 1919 and the sinking of HMS *Royal Oak* twenty years later, cemented the islands' place in world history. Since then the advent of North Sea oil has been carefully managed to maximise the economic impact and minimise the physical. The islands have thus remained attractive to visitors who come to study wildlife, dive on Scapa Flow wrecks, sample the splendid whisky and gaze in wonder at those astonishing archaeological remains, which, after 5,000 years, are still giving Orcadians valuable service.

Traditional Orkney chairs like these have become one of the symbols of the islands. Made using a minimum of wood, to conserve a scarce resource, and with a back of straw ropes, to keep out the draughts, they are highly regarded when new and can command high prices at auction when old.

The shape of Old Kirkwall was determined by the Peedie Sea: not of course the landlocked and landscaped feature that exists today, but as it was hundreds of years ago before it was cut off from the sea. At that time the bay was a larger and wider feature, the thoroughfare that became Broad Street ran beside the shore and the west door of St Magnus Cathedral faced the bay. Over time the head of the bay began to silt up and the sand bar known as the Ayre cut it off from the open sea creating the Peedie Sea. Deliberate infilling reduced its size and buildings erected on the reclaimed land altered the shape of the town, as is evident in this late nineteenth century picture taken from the Ayre. Although it no longer faces the sea, the cathedral remains prominent.

Two cousins, the warlike Hakon and the pious Magnus, each ruled part of Orkney until Magnus was murdered on the orders of Hakon, who became sole ruler. He was followed by his son Paul, but Magnus' nephew Rognvald challenged him, vowing to build a cathedral dedicated to his uncle should he succeed in avenging his death. He did and construction of St Magnus Cathedral, seen here looking from the east, began in 1137, twenty years after the murder of Magnus.

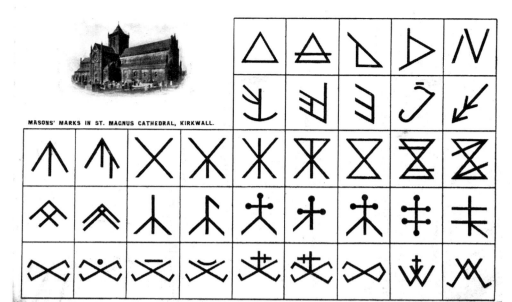

MASONS' MARKS IN ST. MAGNUS CATHEDRAL, KIRKWALL.

The masons of the earliest part of the work are thought to have come from Durham and it is probable that expertise from outside Orkney was employed throughout the 300 or so years it took to complete this magnificent building. As was traditional in their craft, the masons marked the stones they had cut and shaped and this old postcard shows the number and variety of such marks found at the cathedral.

The cathedral survived centuries of religious and political turmoil, ending up, not belonging to the church, but owned by the people of Orkney and administered by their local authority. It has not always fared well structurally. The spire was destroyed by lightning in the late seventeenth century and was replaced by the low pyramid seen in the picture on the facing page. The present spire, seen in this view of the Watergate, was erected as part of extensive remedial work undertaken between 1913 and 1930. The picture was taken about 1930 and shows the ruins of the Bishop's Palace on the left, just beyond the foreground buildings.

The original Bishop's Palace is thought to have been built at much the same time as the early phase of the cathedral. It would have been a simple, rectangular hall-house with storage space on the ground floor and living space above, although nothing of this remains to be seen. The building had apparently fallen into disrepair by 1541 when Robert Reid was appointed as bishop. During his seventeen year tenure Bishop Reid set about reconstructing the palace. He retained the basic design of storage at ground level, but instead of only one floor above there were two and an attic. The bishop also built the distinctive round tower, known as the 'Moosie Too'r', seen in this late nineteenth century picture. The picture also shows perimeter walling and a gateway to the left of the tower which were taken down and rebuilt into the Palace wall to open up the Watergate.

At the start of the seventeenth century Earl Patrick Stewart erected a palace of Renaissance style and flair to equal or surpass any other Scottish building of the time. The riot of colour and decoration inside can only be imagined from the splendour of the remaining architectural features, including the great hall fireplace, said to be the largest in the country, a comment on the Orkney climate perhaps? Not that Earl Patrick enjoyed his palace for long, because he was arrested two or three years after its completion. Subsequently occupied by his nemesis Bishop Law the Earl's Palace was abandoned about 100 years after completion and fell into disrepair. A nineteenth century scheme to renovate it as the Sheriff Court was abandoned and it remained a ruin.

The navy staged an impressive funeral parade on 8 October 1910 to honour 47 year old Warrant Officer, J Thomson, who had been a carpenter on the depot ship, HMS *Blake*. His coffin was placed on a gun carriage at Scapa Pier and from there the procession walked to St Magnus kirkyard where the burial took place after a short service in the cathedral. Three volleys were fired over the grave which was marked, not by a carved headstone, but by a Celtic cross made, appropriately, of wood.

The identity of the deceased in this naval funeral at the St Magnus kirkyard is unknown, but to the left is a headstone erected to the memory of another sailor, Alfred Page, who died on duty in April 1910. He was part of the crew of HMS *Formidable*, one of a large number of ships that had gathered for a fleet exercise. The impressive show of naval might was matched by an equally impressive number of small merchant ships carrying the coal that the fleet leviathans depended on. Able Seaman Page was working in the hold of one of these boats, the *Francis Duncan*, when he was hit by a hoist of sacks and knocked against a bulkhead. With his skull fractured he died almost immediately.

The building in the left foreground of this picture taken from the cathedral tower was the tolbooth. Built in 1740 it was a court house, a prison and the place where the town council conducted its business. It was demolished in 1890 following construction of the new town hall which was erected on the site of the buildings facing camera on the right. They were demolished by the summer of 1884 which helps to date the picture to some time prior to that.

The town hall was built to the designs of architect Thomas S. Peace. On 20 August 1884 the foundation stone was laid by the Earl of Mar and Kellie and the building was completed by 1886. With the town hall on one side and St Magnus Cathedral on the other, this end of Broad Street was the civic and ecclesiastical centre of the town. Between them sat the market cross, a small but significant element of civic infrastucture where proclamations of important news were read out to the townspeople. The old seventeenth century cross, seen here just to the left of centre, was replaced by a replica in 1954 and put in the cathedral for safekeeping.

Castle Street on the right is so-named because there was a castle here, the origins of which may go back to the eleventh century. At that time the Peedie Sea lapped the site which was used in the late fourteenth century by Earl Henry St Clair to build a more substantial structure. In 1614 supporters of Earl Patrick Stewart, led by his son Robert, were besieged in the building by the Earl of Caithness. Following his victory the castle was largely destroyed and the ruin was removed in 1865 to allow the street to be developed. The three-storey building on the corner with Castle Street, reduced to two-storeys by the 1930s, was used for a time by the drapers and outfitters Peace & Low before it became the local branch of the Clydesdale Bank.

With the lamp post in the foreground making Kirkwall look like an urban Narnia, Broad Street is seen here in January 1918 when, in the opinion of elderly Orcadians, the islands were hit by the worst snowstorms since 1855. For weeks heavy snowfalls assailed the islands and with high winds whipping the lying snow into drifts several feet thick, roads were blocked, mail services disrupted, pipes frozen and shortages of milk and meat developed. Pretty, but worrying too!

There are of course many trees in Orkney, but the unusual sight of one growing in the main town's main street created the myth that trees could not grow on the wind-blasted islands and that Albert Street's 'big tree' was the only one. It had in fact been growing in a garden taken over when the road was widened in the nineteenth century and was simply left where it was. It has at times been protected by railings and sparked arguments as to whether or not it should be cut down, but it has survived into the twenty-first century, albeit as a shadow of its former self. Tourism promoters loved it and it appeared in many pictures, some of which may have been processed at Stewart & Heddle's shop where the Kodak signs are a reminder that photography was once an important part of the service provided by the local chemist. Pictures of a different kind were shown at the neighbouring Albert Kinema from 1928 until it was destroyed by fire in 1947.

Stronsay man Peter Shearer started his tailoring business in Kirkwall in 1883 making tweed suits for well-to-do gentlemen, with some clients based as far away as London. The First World War caused a slump in this trade, but when the navy arrived in Scapa Flow so did a large number of new customers. Deftly switching to making officers' uniforms, Peter Shearer also pioneered a new type of coat which became known as the British Warm. Less formal than the regulation uniform greatcoat it proved popular for many years with civilian as well as military users.

Albert Street has long been Kirkwall's principal shopping thoroughfare and although there have been many changes over the years to the names above the shop doors, and in the goods they sell, the street remains a thriving commercial centre. It is seen here at its northern end in 1952 looking toward the junction with Bridge Street.

The point at which Albert Street and Bridge Street merge is known as 'The Brig' because this was the location of a bridge over the Papdale Burn before it was culverted. With the burn thus hidden, the Bridge Street name remained as a source of bewilderment to anyone seeking reasons in an uncertain world. The street is seen here looking from 'The Brig' towards the harbour in 1958.

The little shop to the left of centre in the upper picture is seen here in a picture thought to date from the early 1920s when G. Graham started in business as a butcher. The street furniture of telephone and junction boxes has clearly changed over the years, but the most arresting feature to modern eyes is the display of poultry and wild fowl. The variety of birds is remarkable, but to have raw foodstuffs hanging outside the shop, exposed to dirt and insects, and possibly dripping fluids onto the public street, would give present day health and safety inspectors apoplexy. The hygiene regime inside the shop probably ran to little more than covering the floor with sawdust to absorb anything that might drip on it.

One of the many businesses to operate in Bridge Street over the years was a private lodging house run by an A. Eunson between 1896 and 1911 and by Mrs Eunson up to 1924. Despite being close to the harbour area and its ever changing mix of seafaring strangers, this douce lady ran her boarding house as a temperance establishment.

With Bridge Street to its left and the harbour basin in the right foreground, Kirkwall Hotel stands out proudly in this picture taken soon after the hotel's completion in 1890. Designed by Thomas Smith (T.S.) Peace, it was built as an up-market establishment to cater for the growing number of well-to-do steamer passengers. The pier house, on the left foreground edge, was erected in 1871.

Above: Kirkwall grew as Orkney's principal town because it was the site of the cathedral and not because it had the best harbour. The Peedie Sea served as a beach harbour before it was partly infilled and cut off from the open sea, but is unlikely to have been used by large vessels. Given the town's importance it is probable that some sort of jetty existed before the early nineteenth century when two piers were made to create the harbour. The East Pier, seen in this view from the Kirkwall Hotel, was lengthened in the late nineteenth century to allow larger steam vessels to come alongside.

Below: The ship alongside Kirkwall Pier in this early twentieth century picture is the Orkney Islands Shipping Company's *Orcadia*, a 139 ton steamer that was launched at South Shields in April 1868 and arrived on station four weeks later. She was the second vessel to bear the name and operated as the north isles' steamer up to 1931 with a short interlude in 1884 when she was lengthened by twenty feet and given new engines at Hall, Russell's yard in Aberdeen.

When the *Orcadia* was taken off the north isles service in 1931 she was replaced by a new 221 ton ship, the *Earl Sigurd*, seen on the left of this picture of Kirkwall Pier. She was built at Hall Russell's yard in Aberdeen and proved to be the last steam-driven vessel on Orkney island services. Although the distances she travelled were never long, she once memorably spent 48 fog-bound hours sailing between Westray and Kirkwall. She was replaced in 1962 by a new *Orcadia*, although she remained as back-up until 1969. The ship on the right is the *Amelia*, a 357 ton vessel that started operating between Leith and Kirkwall in 1920 under the ownership of Cooper and Sons, and ended her service in 1955 as part of the 'North Company's' fleet.

The contract to carry mail to Orkney and Shetland was awarded in 1838 to the Aberdeen, Leith, Clyde and Tay Shipping Company. In 1875, as sail gave way to steam, the company name was changed to the North of Scotland & Orkney & Shetland Steam Navigation Company. Their passenger ships continued to serve the islands from both Leith and Aberdeen until *St Ninian*, seen here with Wideford Hill in the background, was withdrawn in 1971.

The schooner *Kathleen Annie* was bound for Newfoundland when she grounded on Muckle Green Holm off Eday in September 1924. Some of her cargo of rectified spirit was taken off allowing her to be refloated and beached off Crow Ness in Kirkwall Bay. HM Customs took charge of the wreck and a freighter named *Leaside* arrived to take off the cargo, but at low tide she could not get alongside and stood off while a drifter, the *Busy Bee*, trans-shipped spirit to her. During this operation, spirit fumes caused a fire to start in the drifter's engine room and although the skipper got his boat clear he could not prevent exploding spirit containers from feeding the fire and destroying the *Busy Bee*. *Kathleen Annie* was later broken up, but a big question remained: at the time of American Prohibition what was the real destination of the schooner's dangerous cargo?

The Kirkwall Junior Sailing Club's annual regatta on Kirkwall Bay in August 1906 featured a race for two-oared boats manned by men from the visiting destroyer flotilla. One of the eight boats led from the start, but its crew misread the course and covered a distance that was about a third longer than their rivals. They were clearly strong rowers, because, despite the error they were not last, but could not catch the crews from HMS *Tyne*, HMS *Down* and HMS *Garry* who were respectively first, second and third.

Photographers in Orkney loved to display their skill and show off the uniqueness of their northern location by taking pictures at midnight in midsummer, like this view of Shore Street. For the modern viewer, it is perhaps the subject matter that is more remarkable because these characterful houses, with their gables presented to the sea, had come to be seen as slums and were demolished many years ago. Since then the shoreline has been altered by land reclamation and the building of the breakwater. Had they survived the houses would have made a splendid backdrop to the marina contained within the harbour extension.

It was rare for Orcadians to get involved in the goings on to the south, but in 1650 about 1,000 islanders were persuaded to join the royalist army led by the Marquis of Montrose. They were routed at the Battle of Carbisdale and their involvement encouraged Oliver Cromwell to send an occupying force to the islands. The soldiers quartered themselves on the islanders and built a fort, some traces of which still existed in the early decades of the twentieth century. It was sited on the promontory to the right of this picture which was taken in 1930. The houses facing the sea are in Cromwell Road, a name that acts as a reminder of this episode in Orkney history.

As well as having plenty of real boats to sail on, some Kirkwalians also enjoyed sailing model yachts, with an annual regatta organised by the Kirkwall Model Yacht Club. When this picture was taken the annual upkeep of the retaining wall and clearance of weeds and rubbish from the pond was paid for by Sir Arthur Bignold. This perhaps accounts for it being known at the time as Bignold Pond, although later generations knew it simply as the Duckie Pond. Sir Arthur also gifted the park and playing fields known as Bignold Park to the town.

Victoria Street retains more in the way of historic architectural features than the more commercial streets, including some interesting dated lintel stones - one on the tall building in the centre of this late nineteenth century picture is from 1679. On the right, where the corner of the building has been angled and corbelled up to the square at first floor level, is a shop where William Johnston conducted business for many years selling coal, manure, slates and general merchandise. The building has since been demolished, creating an open space in front of the Orkney Hotel. Access into the original courtyard here was through an arched pend which can be seen below the lantern in the centre of the picture. The arch has also gone although a stump of masonry remains.

Orkney weather is influenced by the sea. Air flows and ocean currents from the Atlantic keep temperatures up, while the North Sea can cool things down and bring in the fog. Summers are not warm, but winters can be no colder than southern England. Rainfall is significantly less than the Hebrides or the West Highlands of Scotland, and snow falls less often or lies for a shorter time than in northern Scotland, but it does snow, as this picture of West Tankerness Lane shows. It was taken on 16 January 1918 during the severe storms that hit the islands during that month.

With the Bishop's Palace in the centre background, Palace Road is seen here in 1930. To the right is St Magnus Cathedral with its new spire and to the left of centre is the building erected as the Congregational Church in 1876. On the right is a hut-like building where joiner, D.M.Kirkness made church furniture and coffins. It also doubled as the workshop where Reynold Eunson later maintained the tradition of making Orkney chairs.

St Olaf's Episcopal Church and rectory, on the right of this 1930 view of Dundas Crescent, were built in 1875/76 to the designs of architect Alexander Ross. The tower with pyramidal roof was intended from the start, but not added until 1886 when T. S. Peace acted as architect. The stonework of the window in the gable facing the street was also remodelled, and stained glass work representing Faith, Hope and Charity was installed in 1931.

With Coplands Lane in the foreground, this picture taken from the Cathedral about 1880 shows the buildings that later became elements of the Council offices. To the left of centre is the original Kirkwall Grammar School, erected in 1873/74 to the designs of architect T. S. Peace. On the right is the United Presyterian Church, a church that owed its origins to a group of churchmen who broke away from the Established Church of Scotland in 1733. They were concerned about the influence of the state and rich patrons on church affairs, and the need for purity in interpretation of the gospel. They set up what were known as Secession Churches and although these split into a number of smaller factions, they came together again in 1847 to form the United Presbyterian Church. Kirkwall's U.P. church was built at this time. It became known as the Paterson Church, after a long-serving minister, and also the East Church.

The U.P. Church and St Magnus Cathedral are both prominent in this wide view of the town taken from the east in the late nineteenth century. Beyond the fields in the foreground, which have since been filled with housing, is the tree-filled valley of the Papdale Burn with the mid-nineteenth century Papdale Mill to the right. On the extreme left is a house, actually two semi-detached houses, that now sit at the corner of White Street and Willow Road.

A Royal Commission, set up in 1912 to look into housing provision for working people, reported in 1919. That same year, shocked by its conclusions, parliament passed the first of a series of Housing Acts giving local authorities powers to erect public housing. In Kirkwall the first 44 houses to be built under the terms of the act were erected in Willowburn Road. Designed by T. S. Peace and built by contractor John Firth, they comprised a living room, three bedrooms, scullery, bathroom, larder, and coal store. The foundation stone was laid in August 1921 by Lady Smith, wife of Sir Malcolm Smith, MP for Orkney and Shetland, and the first tenants moved in a few months later.

The Carters Park housing is seen beyond the trees in the valley of the Papdale Burn, in this picture taken from the U. P. Church. In the foreground is the house known as Willowdene with beside it what appears to be the nursery run by Robert and Sidney Leitch. They donated a few hundred trees to the burgh to mark the Silver Jubilee of King George V in 1935. Two years later the Coronation of King George VI was marked by another gift of trees, this time by Dean of Guild, P. C. Flett. The trees were planted by school children and members of the town council. The backs of houses in Willow Road are seen beyond Willowdene and the two little cottages next to the nursery appear to be under construction.

The Free Church in King Street was erected in 1892/93 for a congregation that had worshiped in temporary accommodation after it had broken away from the Established Church of Scotland at the time of the Disruption. The dispute, in 1843, arose out of a growing concern over the role of the state in the affairs of the Church of Scotland and also the position given to patrons who, as powerful landowners, were able to appoint ministers against the wishes of parishioners. Nearly half of all churchmen and their congregations walked out, a move that substantially weakened the existing parochial structure of local government and led to major changes in social legislation. The Free Church amalgamated with the United Presbyterian Church in 1900 to form the United Free Church and this reunited with the Church of Scotland in 1929, moves that created a surfeit of church buildings, but the King Street Church survived to become a church hall.

This photograph looking along King Street toward Queen Street appears to have been taken about 1880, before the Free Church was built.

Old Scapa Road is seen here looking towards High Street in a picture taken in 1930 from the intersection with Nicolson Street. Just out of picture to the left is the so-called 'County Home', a complex of sheltered housing, day centre and care accommodation for elderly people.

This photograph of Glaitness Road was almost certainly taken on the same day in 1930 as the upper picture. It has been taken from a spot close to Glaitness House, just out of picture on the left, and looks back toward the junction of High Street and Old Scapa Road. Housing has since been built on the vacant ground in the right foreground.

Footballers in Orkney originally played rugby, but about 1890 a young Kirkwalian, Jackie Dearness, returned to his home town to take up a job with the Orkney Herald newspaper. Prior to that he had been working in Wick where he had been introduced to the delights of Association Football, and through his efforts a local team known as Thorfinn F.C. was formed, with Jackie as its captain. This team photograph, apparently taken on the same day as the game in the lower picture, appears to show the Thorfinn team for season 1907-08. A few years later, in 1910, the club's name was changed to Kirkwall City, but later reverted to Thorfinn.

After their formation, Thorfinn played a number of games against the local rugby team, St Magnus, which must have been something of a spectacle with each trying to adapt to the others' rules, but soon St Magnus. also switched to the round ball game which grew in popularity in the islands. Games were played against teams from Stromness, Wick, Thurso and the navy, and in 1908 the Milne Cup competition was instituted against the Shetland Islands, with Thorfinn players featuring strongly in Orkney teams. In the early days the park was a rented field and players changed in the shelter of the dyke. The field in this picture appears to be at Pickaquoy, appropriately close to the site of the present day 'Picky' Centre.

The ceremony to open the extension of the Orkney Golf Club's course to eighteen holes, in July 1927, was attended by a large number of people, although club captain, James Flett, could not be there and his place was taken by vice-captain, Provost White. After the speeches, in which it was noted that this was the most northerly eighteen hole course in Britain, Miss Davidson, the ladies captain, was gifted a new driver and invited to inaugurate the course. Mindful of potential embarrassment, however, she was allowed to use her familiar old club and with it sent a 150 yard drive down the first fairway. Thereafter mixed foursomes were played over the whole course.

Situated adjacent to the bowling green, Kirkwall's new tennis court was regarded as well-sheltered and easy to reach. It was opened on the afternoon of 18 May 1927 and although fewer people turned out for its opening than for that of the golf course extension they made up for it with enthusiasm, playing a number of games and breaking only for a welcome cup of tea.

Two sixteen seater buses owned by William Grant of the Castle Hotel and operated by W. R. Tullock as the Orkney Motor Express, began a service between Kirkwall and Stromness in July 1905. It was sufficiently successful to encourage the operators to put on a 43 seater double decker bus the following year, although they may have regretted doing so when Stromness Town Council sued them for the cost of a gas lamp knocked down on the vehicle's first visit to the town. The mishap did not, however, impede the development of services with many other buses, and operators opening up a variety of routes and services. Many of these have since withered in the face of competition from the private car.

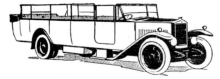

Orcadians were quick to recognise the value of motor vehicles and a number of garages or workshops were set up to serve the growing demand. One of these was Leslie and Leonard in Junction Road, who had been selling and maintaining bicycles before adding cars and lorries to their business. The lorry on the right is sporting the BS letters given to all Orkney-owned motors under the first British vehicle registration system.

Kirkwall's first electricity generating station was a steel-framed, corrugated-iron building equipped with three sets of 65 brake horsepower semi-diesel or gas oil engines. It was opened in February 1924 when Mrs John White, wife of the Provost, switched on the current, turning on lights in the building itself, at the pier and the town hall. Mrs White was given an electric lamp as a memento of the occasion. A new power station, built on a site between the Peedie Sea and Great Western Road, superseded the old one in 1951.

Partial infilling and landscaping of the Peedie Sea, and the building of a more substantial road, means that the Ayre is no longer the narrow causeway seen in this late nineteenth century picture taken from the Kirkwall Hotel. In the right foreground is the West Pier, opposite the seventeenth century grain store known as the Girnel. In the distance is the nineteenth century Ayre Mill which was driven by the power of the tides moving through the Oyce, the narrow gap between the Peedie Sea and the bay. The wheel could be adjusted to cope with variations in the height and direction of the water flow. This unique arrangement, introduced in 1839, was later superseded by steam but ironically, in these more environmentally conscious times, Orkney is again at the forefront of efforts to generate power from the force of the tides.

Another image early photographers liked to convey was the battering Orkney could experience from the sea. In this picture, it is the Ayre that is in the eye of the storm as waves crash across it into the Peedie Sea. The large building getting wet is the Ayre Hotel which was originally erected in the late eighteenth century as two separate dwellings.

Travelling shops were a feature of Orkney life, providing a lifeline service to rural and remote communities. Often, instead of just selling goods at the roadside, they traded merchandise for farm produce and could return to Kirkwall as heavily loaded as they had left. The principal travelling shop operator was Robert Garden and one of the main commodities he dealt in was eggs which his vans brought back to Kirkwall for packing and export.

Robert Garden also used the 71 ton steamer *Cormorant* to carry goods between Orkney and little harbours in the north or west of Scotland. She had been operating in Orkney waters for four years when Robert Garden bought her in 1897 and she remained four years after he sold her in 1934. In that time she acquired a reputation for getting into trouble, but always escaping to sail another day.

Caldale on the Old Finstown Road became a base during the First World War for airships and observation balloons, known as kite balloons. These were filled with hydrogen at Caldale and taken by road to be loaded onto naval vessels. While at sea, a ship could let out the balloon, attached to a cable, up to heights of 1,000 feet, so that an observer on board could report on what he had seen. Balloons were also flown from ships at anchor in Scapa Flow to hamper any attack by enemy bombers.

With Kirkwall Harbour facing north it was often easier for ships approaching from the south to use Scapa Pier. The ship in the background, apparently leaving the pier, is the Pentland Firth steamer *St Ola*. The pier had the disadvantage of being somewhat exposed to the south west and could be affected by a swell in southerly winds, but with modern extensions it is still used by boats servicing oil tankers in Scapa Flow. The photographer has unfortunately framed his shot too tightly to include the Scapa Distillery on the far shore, to the right. At the time the picture was taken, three distilleries operated on the islands, Scapa, one in Stromness that produced a whisky called 'Old Orkney', and Highland Park.

HIGHLAND PARK DISTILLERY, ORKNEY

ESTABLISHED 1798

HIGHLAND — PARK DISTILLERY. ORKNEY. T.K.
Simmath

JAMES GRANT & CO., Proprietors,
Distillers of the FINEST PURE - - MALT WHISKY - -

Highland Park whisky has become one of the better known symbols of Orkney, carrying the name across the world. The distillery was established in 1798 on, if the stories are true, the site of an illicit still. It produces a distinctively flavoured pure malt whisky, the result of turning the grain on the malting floor by hand and drying it over smoke from a peat fire laced with heather faggots, with the peat cut from the distillery's own moor at Hobbister. Add to that pure, clear, Orkney spring water and cool Orkney air and the result, matured in sherry oak casks, is sublime.

There is an almost timeless sense of peace and tranquility about this picture of a man walking into town along a country road, except that the picture was taken in 1940 when peace and tranquility, especially on fortress Orkney, were in very short supply. Published with the title 'On The Road to Kirkwall', the actual highway is the main road to and from Deerness and the airport. The little cottage in the left foreground no longer sits in glorious isolation, with modern housing having spread out from Kirkwall to almost surround it.

The technological advances available by the early twentieth century may have been readily adopted in and around Kirkwall, but in country areas the old ways lingered on. The contrast is perhaps most vividly illustrated by the way photographers, using sophisticated equipment, set out to record a way of life in cottages that had remained largely unchanged for centuries. The upper of these two pictures, taken at Netherby, Deerness, shows a somewhat sanitised interior. In the background are box beds with panelled front and sliding doors. Spinning wheels sit amongst the scattered chairs and the photographer, Tom Kent, has artfully added a woman sitting in an Orkney chair, knitting. This has been done with such skill the join is hard to detect. Perhaps the most interesting element of the picture is the central fire. It has been made up against a large stone, a feature that had long since evolved into the more substantial wall, known as the back, seen in the lower picture. The arrangement of hooks and chains above the fire could be lengthened or shortened by hitching a link up or down depending on how much heat was needed for cooking. This interior looks more primitive and cramped with what appears to be another bed made up in front of the box bed in the background.

The typical 'but and ben' cottage housed not just the crofter and his family, but their animals as well. There was often only one entrance to the building, at the but-end where the animals were kept and people had to pass through it to get to the living area. There was direct access between the two areas even in cottages which had a separate entry to the ben-end. The door in the background of this cottage interior at Orphir probably leads to where the byre, stable and barn were once located. The picture looks from behind the fire and shows the usual scatter of simple furniture and utensils. Part of the roof structure can be seen although whether it had an aperture through which the smoke from the fire escaped, or if it simply percolated through the thatch, is not known. The fire 'back' has been built with a step, like an embryonic room divider.

The stepped fire back is also evident in this cottage at Kirbuster. Some attempt has been made to decorate the interior with wallpaper, but despite this concession to modernity the fire is still set on an open hearth, the furniture is rudimentary and there is a cruisie lamp on the wall. This type of lamp had two trays, the upper of which was filled with oil and had a wick laid in it. Drips from the burning wick were caught by the lower tray.

The Holm Parish Church, a couple of miles east of St Mary's, was originally built in 1814 as a meeting house of one of the Secession Churches. Following the formation of the United Free Church in 1900 it became known as the Holm East Church, but when the United Free Presbytery of Orkney decided to make it the parish church they met some active opposition. The protests began with the church windows being broken, but with the Presbytery sticking to its decision their opponents burned the church down in the early hours of 29 February 1920. These pictures show it soon after the fire. Such vandalism was only ever going to harden opinion and the building was reinstated at a cost greatly reduced by voluntary work given by parishioners, including the architect. It was rededicated as the parish church in August 1924. The manse, which dates from the same period as the church, can be seen in the background.

Graemshall, to the east of St Mary's, was built in two phases in the 1870s and 1890s, replacing an earlier laird's house and courtyard. The owner, Alexander Graeme, and his wife Margaret Neale carried out the design work, incorporating some features from the earlier buildings and including a small chapel. For a time the house was used to display the Norwood Collection, a privately assembled collection of porcelain, pottery, lustreware, silver and other antiques.

Orcadians are often described as farmers who fish and Shetlanders as fishermen who farm, but as with all such generalisations there are exceptions and for a time one of those was St Mary's Holm. To begin with a small community developed around the ferries that operated between here and the islands to the south, but in the 1830s houses were built and men were encouraged to move in and exploit the abundant cod and ling fisheries. The industry thrived and a deep water pier was built in the 1870s. It was later extended and by the end of the nineteenth century the emphasis was no longer on cod, but had shifted to herring. St Mary's ceased to be a viable fishing port when access to fishing grounds to the east was first obstructed and then closed by the measures taken to protect the Royal Navy's anchorage in Scapa Flow.

Fishing boats were required by The British White Herring Act of 1860 to have a registration number painted in white on a black background on each bow, as is evident on the foreground yawl drawn up on the shore at St Mary's in this early twentieth century picture. The number also had to be shown clearly on the sails. Ports were allocated identifying letters and each port then issued the number. Only two Scottish ports were marked with a single letter, K for Kirkwall and A for Aberdeen, most, like Lerwick (LK), were identified with two letters, but three letters were used for a few places including SMH for St Margaret's Hope.

The Holm Community Centre was set up in a former drill hall in St Mary's, seen here on the left. It had been built in 1881 for use by the men of No. 6 Company, 1st. Orkney, Royal Garrison Artillery Volunteers. When the hall became surplus to requirements, just before the First World War, it was purchased privately and gifted to the community. After the Second World War the Holm Community Association took over the hall as a community centre. It became popular for dances, concerts, film shows, sales of work and all those other activities that glue a community together. A modern facility has since been erected on the site.

The community centre's hall and the house that was purchased to extend the facility are on the left of this view looking along Back Road, St Mary's. The Nissen hut seen on the right and in the upper picture is one of many former wartime buildings still evident around the islands.

Orkney's volunteer soldiers, like all such units around the country, gathered for a period of intensive training at an annual camp, like this one at Weyland Farm in 1908. Postcards were quickly produced so that the men could send news home: this one was sent to a mother in Rendall by her son who was 'getting on splendidly and liking camp grand'. The Royal Garrison Artillery operated heavy guns, unlike the light, mobile, field guns of other artillery units, so from an early date men on Orkney were learning about the kind of weapons that would later be used to guard the entrances to Scapa Flow. With the modern Territorial Army base located at Weyland, the area remains important to volunteer forces. Two imposing old cannon placed outside maintain a link with the gunners of the old Royal Garrison Artillery.

The gunners manning Holm Battery found the job of guarding Scapa Flow dull. Charlie, one of the men in this picture, had received a letter from his cousin, but delayed his reply because, as he wrote in May 1915, 'I really have no news'. The letter continued with comments like: 'I am still stuck out here and likely to remain' and 'you have no idea how I appreciate a letter, it is so monotonous here'.

Scapa Flow was identified as a suitable naval anchorage in 1812, but not thought about seriously until the decade before the First World War when the Royal Navy used it for exercises. With war imminent, the navy arrived in force, but because nothing had been done to protect the ships at anchor defences had to be hastily installed. A submarine got close to breaching these early in the war, but it was spotted and forced to surrender. A nervous navy requisitioned a number of old ships and sank them in the vulnerable eastern entrances to render them un-navigable. This picture shows a group of these partially submerged 'block ships', as they were known, in Holm Sound.

In hindsight it seems astonishing that, after the First World War, the navy dismantled some of their defences and neglected others. The result was, that at the start of the Second World War, a submarine was famously able to get into Scapa Flow and sink the battleship HMS *Royal Oak*. Block ships were again used to close the gaps, but in March 1940 Winston Churchill approved the construction of solid barriers. Huge nets filled with boulders were initially sunk on the line of the proposed barrier and large concrete blocks were placed around and on top of these to create the solid structure. The Churchill Barriers, known locally as just 'The Barriers', not only closed the four eastern openings, but effectively made the islands to the south of St Mary's into part of the mainland.

Burray became Orkney's principal southern fishing port during the great herring boom that started in the late nineteenth century. The season began around midsummer and lasted until August during which time gutters, coopers and fishermen flocked to the island turning it into a hive of activity as can be seen from this early twentieth century picture of the fishing station on Burray Pier. Some of the boats taking part in this glut were local, but most came from elsewhere. The industry peaked just before the First World War, but as at St Mary's, the Scapa Flow defences wrecked any prospect of a revival. Fishing's legacy is a former herring store converted into a hotel for the new boom industry, tourism.

The attractive village of St Margaret's Hope, with houses dating back to the seventeenth century and facing gable on to the sea, is the principal community on South Ronaldsay, although its importance was diminished to some extent when the island was connected to the mainland by 'The Barriers'. It is also the location of a unique folk custom: the Boys' Ploughing Match and Festival of the Horse. Children dressed in gaily decorated clothes represent the horses while boys, using miniature ploughs, some of which are very old, compete to see who can make the straightest furrow in the sand.

The herring industry made use of the pier to the west of St Margaret's Hope although the industry on South Ronaldsay never reached the same scale as at Burray. Built in the nineteenth century the 100 metre long pier was also used by small cargo steamers, as can be seen in this picture, but not by the regular mail steamers operating between Scotland and Orkney. Modern ferries, sailing to and from Gill's Bay in Caithness, have given the pier a new lease of life.

Instead of calling at the St Margaret's Hope pier the mail steamers stood off Hoxa Head and were met by small boats which carried people, luggage and mail between the ship and the shore. The transfer from the larger vessel to a small sailing craft could be a hazardous and uncomfortable activity for some people, even in calm weather. Some improvement came in 1912 when John McBeth introduced the six ton motor boat *Winsome*, seen here with the *St Nicholas* in the background. Renamed *Hoxa Head* soon after coming on station, she carried mails between St Margaret's Hope and Burray and the steamers, and also operated a regular weekly passenger service between St Margaret's Hope and Scapa. She performed these tasks in all weathers for twenty years.

When South Ronaldsay was still an island, the appearance of a motor car in St Margaret's Hope must have been a remarkable sight, so much so that a picture postcard was published of this one at the East End. Curiously bearing a Moray registration plate rather than one from Orkney, it is seen squeezing through the narrow gap between William Sinclair's shop-cum-post and telegraph office and the steps leading to and from Church Road.

Church Road takes its name from St Margaret's Church, which can be seen at the top of the hill in this view looking up from the junction with Back Road. The building was erected in the mid nineteenth century as a United Presbyterian Church and is believed to incorporate stones taken from an earlier building that was demolished at the time of the reunification of the Secession Churches in 1847.

When it became clear that the bodies of those killed during the First World War would not be brought home for burial, people throughout Britain sought to mark their deaths in a communal way. Orcadians responded quickly, erecting a host of parish memorials. The South Ronaldsay memorial, surmounted by a figure of a Seaforth Highlander carved out of Corstorphine stone by Edinburgh sculptor Alexander Carrick, was unveiled on 21 August 1921. The ceremony was performed by a Miss Sutherland on behalf of her mother, who had lost two sons, killed, and a third severely wounded in the conflict.

Unlike the local vernacular dwellings, which seek shelter from the elements, Roeberry House, a large Victorian villa dating from the 1860s, was built to take advantage of the fine views, which means of course that it also stands out prominently in the South Ronaldsay landscape. Known locally as 'The Castle' and surrounded by walled gardens, it is seen here prior to the addition of a conservatory. The Sands o'Right beach, where the Boys' Ploughing Match takes place, is close to Roeberry House.

Situated on the southern shore of Widewall Bay and with a clear view across the water to Roeberry House, the hamlet of Herston was developed in the nineteenth century as a fishing village. The industry here never achieved the scale of St Mary's or Burray and many of the houses have since become pleasant dwellings. The only evidence of fishing is provided by the remains of some boats lying on the shore in front of the foreground enclosure, itself overgrown and derelict.

The contrast is stark between the conspicuous wealth required to impose a building like Roeberry House on the landscape, and the equally obvious poverty of this little cottage blending into its surroundings. The woman at the door was Margaret Brown, said to be the last of the cottars on South Ronaldsay.

The little lighthouse on Hoxa Head was one of a number of similar cast-iron, gas powered lights designed by David A. Stevenson and erected at the start of the twentieth century. First lit in 1901 it was intended to make the passage through the Sound of Hoxa easier and safer, but during two world wars the military authorities took measures to ensure that, for some ships at least, this stretch of water was much less welcoming. An artillery battery was sited on Hoxa Head during the First World War, which may explain why these men are trying to control a small boat in difficult conditions below the cliffs, and in 1940 the Balfour Battery was erected close to the lighthouse, to guard the defensive boom placed between South Ronaldsay and Flotta. Hoxa Head light was dismantled in 1996 and taken to the lighthouse museum at Kinnaird Head, Fraserburgh. It was replaced by a beacon.

This group of men, described as a 'working party' in a note written on the reverse of the picture, appears to have been engaged on construction or maintenance of one of the many naval installations established on Flotta during both world wars, although a reference to 'the front' places this picture firmly during the First World War. The tone of the note and somewhat casual adherence to uniform suggests that the men may have been Orcadian reservists. Peacetime solitude had replaced wartime activity for only a couple of decades before Occidental Oil recognised Flotta's strategic value and set up their terminal on the island in the 1970s, but despite hosting this symbol of modern life, Flotta's landscape still bears the scars of its military past.

On a wild, dark, snow-laden night in February 1906 some fishermen in South Walls saw the lights of a ship where no ship should have been. She was the *Dinnington*, a 366 ton collier whose captain had tried to gain the shelter of Longhope, but had instead grounded on Switha. Two of the crew were washed away and drowned, but the other nine got ashore. The South Walls men put out in their yawl to Switha, found no-one, went to Flotta and back to Switha before locating the half-drowned men. It was an heroic rescue in dreadful conditions for which the RNLI awarded six silver medals, despite it not being carried out by a lifeboat.

A lifeboat has been stationed at Longhope since 1874 and its crews, like these men with the *Thomas McCann*, have attended numerous incidents without attracting the attention of the wider public, but in March 1969 all that changed. In appalling weather, the Liberian registered *Irene*, off course and almost out of fuel, had gone aground. She was on the east side of South Ronaldsay although at the time no-one knew where she was, so both Kirkwall and Longhope lifeboats were launched, but in the huge seas the Longhope boat, the *TGB*, capsized with the loss of her crew of eight. It was a devastating blow for the scattered community, compounded by the reality that the *Irene's* crew were rescued by a shore-based team who got a line aboard the stricken ship.

A memorial to the tragic loss of the Longhope lifeboat was erected in Osmondwall cemetery where, almost fifty years earlier in October 1921, local people had witnessed the unveiling of the South Walls War Memorial. The ceremony began with a service at the parish church after which people walked in the solemn procession depicted here to the older part of the cemetery where the nine foot high granite Celtic cross had been set up on a base of Melsetter freestone. To the strains of Lord Lovat's Lament played by the Kirkwall Pipe Band, and with a naval guard of honour, Thomas Middlemore unveiled the memorial.

The Walls part of the South Walls name should be more properly spelled as 'Waas', which in old Norse refers to the bays and inlets that indent the shore. 'Hop', in old Norse, means a single bay and forms part of the name of the principal South Walls settlement, Longhope. It sits on the southern shore of the four mile long bay, also known as Longhope, which is seen here beyond the village pier. The pier was formerly busy with fishing boats and a ferry over to North Walls and during the First World War the bay was heavily used by the Royal Navy. The Admiral commanding the fleet in the Orkney and Shetland Islands had his base set up at Longhope Hotel overlooking the pier.

A century before the Royal Navy scrabbled to turn Scapa Flow into a safe fleet anchorage, similarly hurried arrangements were made to protect Longhope. With French and American privateers preying on lone ships the navy sought to gather them at Longhope and escort them across the Atlantic in convoys. To protect the ships while they rode at anchor a Martello Tower was built on each of the headlands flanking the bay. Surmounted with a gun, these towers, their shape redolent of ancient Pictish brochs, were modelled on a small fortification that had given the Royal Navy a hard time at Cape Mortella in Corsica. Completed in 1813 and 1814 those on Orkney never fired a shot in anger, but should have acted as a warning to the Admiralty that Scapa Flow was a valuable, but vulnerable base. Longhope village grew up around all this activity in the early nineteenth century and three of its principal elements, the Customs House, South Walls School and the general store are seen in these pictures believed to date from the 1920s.

Melsetter House at the head of Longhope is widely regarded as one of Orkney's finest large country houses. Originally an eighteenth century laird's house it was bought in the 1890s by a wealthy industrialist from Birmingham who commissioned the architect W. R. Lethaby to remodel it. The result was a sensitive amalgam of local materials and traditions, with the arts and crafts style of William Morris. Some of the stained glass chapel windows were made by Morris' company, based on designs by the great Pre-Raphaelite artists Edward Burne-Jones and Ford Maddox-Brown. The little pavilion with the flag, on the left, was a tea room, tucked into the corner of the eighteenth century walled garden to balance a doocot at the opposite corner. W. R. Lethaby also remodelled Hoy Lodge, an eighteenth century laird's house at the north end of Hoy.

The northern and western coasts of Hoy present a formidable bulwark of high cliffs against which rolling Atlantic waves pound incessantly. This is not a shore that a mariner in difficulties would be pleased to see because the only place along it that might offer any refuge is Rackwick, where a small crofting community clung to the slopes of Ward Hill ekeing a living out of the harsh environment. The crofters also made the most of their location by going out to fish in the small Orkney yoles seen here drawn up on the beach of sand and huge sea-rounded boulders. As a crofting community Rackwick dwindled to a population of one before its attractions as a holiday retreat led to the reinstatement of some abandoned houses.

Hoy, the high island, is at its highest point, Ward Hill, 1,550 feet above sea level and much of the landscape resembles the rough, upland terrain of Highland Scotland, as this picture of the Dwarfie Stane shows. Sitting close to the road between Rackwick and Linksness, the stone is perhaps the most extraordinary of Orkney's ancient monuments. It consists of a burial chamber with two small side chambers hollowed out of a single large rock. That this was done using stone tools some time before 2000 B.C. has led to some wild flights of fantasy as to its origins. More sober minded archaeologists have also struggled to explain it, to some extent because the boulder used to block the entrance was removed long ago and any contents taken away. Nevertheless, the stone still attracts visitors as this 1930s picture of a couple, clad for the hills, shows.

The shadow of World War Two was beginning to lift when this picture was taken of the post office at the north end of Hoy where such a facility had operated since 1879. Opening a post office was probably the easy bit, collecting and delivering the mail in the more remote parts of the island, like Rackwick, was more challenging. A cart fitted with two large spoked wheels and drawn by an ox was used to do this in the late nineteenth and early twentieth centuries. It may have been unsophisticated, but was probably better than the carts commonly used on the island and its neighbours Graemsay and Flotta. Known variously as sleds, hurlies or lorries these little box-like vehicles, with four small solid or flat-spoked wheels, were also ox-drawn.

When the Royal Navy based its Grand Fleet at Scapa Flow during the First World War it spent much of the time waiting for an opportunity to engage the enemy, but there was only one major clash, the inconclusive Battle of Jutland in 1916. Then in late November 1918, following the cessation of hostilities, 74 surrendered ships of the German Hochseeflotte (High Seas Fleet) sailed under escort into internment in Scapa Flow. They lay there, at anchor, through the winter of 1918/19, while the terms of the armistice were thrashed out.

The five battle cruisers, eleven battleships, eight light cruisers and fifty torpedo-boat destroyers were manned by skeleton crews who were not allowed ashore; if life at Scapa Flow was grim for the men of the Royal Navy, it was infinitely worse for the German sailors. The men lived in cramped conditions initially with poor rations, they were idle, bored and ill-disciplined. They did not believe they had been defeated and, so while Orcadians took trips in small boats to gawp at them and the allies wrangled over their fate, the Germans took matters into their own hands. On 21 June 1919, with the the Royal Navy out on exercise, they scuttled their own ships. The torpedo-destroyers, tucked in between the islands of Rysa and Fara, were the last to receive the order, so returning British ships were able to stop some of them sinking, but most of the great capital ships, anchored in deeper water, went down. A few, like Seiner Majestat Schiff (SMS) *Hindenburg* (above) and the capsized cruiser (below), still showed above the surface, a silent reproach to the complacent bickering allies.

In the early 1920s some enterprising local operators recovered some destroyers and metal from accessible ships, but in 1924 a much larger salvage operation was begun by the firm of Cox and Danks. The name of the tug on the right combines one of the partner's names with the material the company dealt in, iron. Working from a base at Lyness they started with the remaining destroyers and had some early failures, but soon developed an expertise in raising the sunken vessels. From the smaller vessels Cox and Danks graduated to the capital ships with the battlecruiser SMS *Moltke* the first of these to be refloated, in June 1927. The picture shows the cruiser SMS *Bremse* alongside the salvors' floating platform in September 1929.

A new company, Metal Industries Ltd., took over the salvage work in 1932, and eventually all but twelve of the sunk ships were raised, the last, SMS *Derflinger*, was brought to the surface in August 1939, but not scrapped until after the Second World War. She is seen here breaking the surface in a rush of compressed air and water. The mast-like objects projecting from her hull are air locks which the salvors fitted to the upturned hull to gain access and prepare the vessel for raising.

The Royal Navy left Scapa Flow after the First World War, but hurried back just before the outbreak of World War Two. They adopted Lyness as their base, calling it HMS *Prosperine*. It grew rapidly into a large complex of buildings, storage tanks, piers and wharfs, many of which were completed only a year or two before activities at the base began to be scaled down. It was decommissioned in 1957 and has since been made into an interpretation centre.

Orkney, a long way from the navy's usual flesh-pot, port-town bases, was a culture shock for many of the service personnel, and presumably for the civilian contractors employed in bulding the Scapa Flow base. The experience was described by Captain Hamish Blair RN in his famously undiplomatic poem, 'Bloody Orkney': *'This town's a bloody cuss, No bloody trains, no bloody bus, And no one cares for bloody us, In bloody Orkney'*. There was a cinema: *'The bloody flicks are bloody old'*, and some social facilities: *'Everything's so bloody dear, A bloody bob for bloody beer'*, although these pictures of the Officer's Club show that the men did manage to create some entertainment of their own.

The Vikings had recognised the value of Houton Bay as a harbour and so when the Royal Navy started to use Scapa Flow it was inevitable that the peaceful early twentieth century farming scene in the upper picture would be transformed. Instead of crops, accommodation huts started to grow across the hillside and a seaplane base, seen in the lower picture, was established. After the First World War the great capital ships of the interned German fleet were anchored outside the bay, so visitors flocked to Houton to see them, and flocked back again to see where they had sunk. The upturned hull of SMS *Markgraf* and some of the destroyers beached on the island of Cava can be seen in the distance in the lower picture. The value of the bay was also recognised when North Sea oil was discovered, but that transient industry's blandishments were resisted and Houton saved from another bout of despoliation.

Completed about 1846 and subsequently altered, Swanbister House was one of many improvements made to the estate when it was acquired by Archer Fortescue, a man whose name was as out-of-place in Orkney as the huntin', shootin', fishin' way of life he brought with him from Devon.

Orphir is well known for the remains of St Nicholas Church, a unique round church dating from the early twelfth century. Still largely intact in the mid eighteenth century it was partly demolished and robbed of stone to build a new parish church alongside. That church building has since been demolished and the Free Church building, erected in 1885/86, has become the parish church. This former manse, which sits on the hillside beside the Scorradale Road, is therefore one of the least remarkable ecclesiastical buildings in Orphir, but it does enjoy a spectacular view of Scapa Flow.

Stromness, a long thin town stretched out along the shore of a bay known as Hamnavoe, is protected from the worst of the weather to the east by the small tidal islands, the Holms, and to the west by high ground. The view across Stromness from the hill known as Brinkie's Brae is one that has attracted photographers since the invention of the camera. The one who took this picture did so before the Free Church was built in 1890, giving the picture a date some time in the 1880s.

This picture, also taken from Brinkie's Brae, but from a spot a little to the south of the upper view, shows the former Stromness Academy. Stromness had two early schools run by the churches, but these were closed after the passing of the Education Act in 1872 and the pupils transferred to a new school. This was added to in 1884 and 1896, and it was raised to secondary school status in the early twentieth century before being extended again in 1912. The school was largely rebuilt in 1937 when it was renamed Stromness Academy. The building was utilised as a community centre following the construction of the new Academy, on a new site, in 1988.

With its protected harbour Stromness has always been a port, although its growth as a town is comparatively recent. It owes much to the use by eighteenth and nineteenth century shipping going north-about through the Pentland Firth in preference to facing the attentions of hostile Dutch or French warships in the southern North Sea and English Channel. With Kirkwall's harbour facing out to the North Sea and so not as useful, Stromness was better situated for vessels plying the Atlantic. It also became a base for the Hudson's Bay Company, which recruited heavily in Orkney, and for whalers seeking crew for their long voyages to distant grounds.

Stromness was also well placed to cash in on the great herring boom of the late nineteenth and early twentieth century. The season only lasted for a couple of months during the summer, but in that time the town's population was swelled by a huge influx of itinerant fish trade workers. The herring boom peaked about 1905 and was over by the outbreak of the First World War, but Stromness has continued to operate as a fishing port for other species.

The 231 ton *St Ola* is one of the most fondly remembered boats to operate across the Pentland Firth. Known affectionately as the grand old lady she was built in 1892 and remained in service until 1951 when she was replaced by a new *St Ola*. It was a long time for a small vessel to operate in such difficult waters, a testimony to her robust construction at the Aberdeen yard of Hall Russell and to the skill of her crews. The story told on the back of this picture is typical: 'owing to indifferent tides we made wide sweeps around the coast… ran in at Scapa at 11.15 pm, then off round the main island to Stromness and arrived at 1.00 am after a five and half hour trip. The sea was not too bad, although there was a heavy swell and what with rain and wind it was not too agreeable'. Just another crossing for the *St Ola*.

At the pier in this picture is the 920 ton *St Rognvald* which operated as the weekend boat from Aberdeen and on the run known as the 'west side' route to Scalloway in Shetland. She was built at Hall Russell's Aberdeen yard in 1901 to replace a ship of the same name wrecked the previous year on Burgh Head, Stronsay. Like the *St Ola* (above) she could be delayed by sea conditions, most famously in August 1931 when, with 200 passengers on board, she ran into one bank of fog after another and took 72 hours to complete a scheduled twelve hour journey.

A lifeboat has been stationed at Stromness since 1867 when a boathouse and slip was set up at Ness. A new boathouse and slip were built in 1901 and eight years later the first motor-driven boat was put on station. Another new boathouse and slip was needed to accommodate her replacement by a type of boat that incorporated many features suggested by the Stromness men. Named with the initials of the five donors who paid for her, the *J.J.K.S.W.*, seen here, arrived in March 1928 and had already carried out a major rescue before being officially christened. By the time she was replaced in 1955 she had been launched 92 times and rescued 139 people.

The *J.J.K.S.W.* was officially named by Prince George in June 1928. He arrived on board a naval pinnace in bright sunshine and, accompanied by the official party, made his way along the beflagged and decorated street to the boat-house. After naming the new lifeboat he presented the RNLI's Challenge Shield to Helen F. F. Scott of Burness School, Sanday, who had won the Institution's annual schools essay competition. After lunch the prince was greeted on the steps of Stromness Hotel by some young ladies selling RNLI flags to raise funds. He donated some money to Ella Sutherland while Jessie Slater pinned a flag on his coat.

Much of the Stromness waterfront was built in the eighteenth and nineteenth centuries with houses and piers jutting out from the shore so that boats could come alongside as close to houses and warehouses as possible. One of the most popular images for early photographers was the windows at the backs of houses in Dundas Street from which a fishing line could be dropped into the water at high tide to catch silcocks or saithe.

Stromness Harbour may be sheltered, but it is not deep and piers had to be built for the ships shuttling back and forth between it and mainland Scotland. This view shows the South Pier on the left and the old North Pier on the right. It was reconstructed in 1922 to suit the requirements of a company called Thornley Binders which planned to make briquettes (small blocks of fuel) using locally harvested seaweed, and dross coal from Wales. Despite the investment, the company went bust and no briquettes were ever made, which prompted the harbour authorities to repossess the pier. Dominating the picture is the Stromness Hotel, built to the designs of architect Samuel Baikie in 1901. To the right are the late nineteenth century Town House and Masonic Hall buildings.

Running parallel with the shoreline is 'the street', the main thoroughfare of the town which changes name a number of times along its length. This picture taken about 1960 outside the post office, looks north along Victoria Street toward the pier head and John Street.

The same section of Victoria Street as in the upper picture is shown here, with a corner of the harbour master's house at the head of South Pier on the left. The old buildings beyond it on the left must have been replaced soon after the picture was taken around the turn of the nineteenth and twentieth centuries. Like most ports Stromness was noted for its pubs, but in November 1920 the town voted to go dry under the terms of the Temperance (Scotland) Act. People could still obtain a drink in a hotel if they had it with a meal and some hoteliers were very creative in their interpretation of what constituted a meal, but despite these arrangements, and a couple of attempts to reverse the decision, the town remained without pubs until 1948.

One of the most prominent buildings in the town is the Free Church, with its distinctive octagonal spire it was erected to the designs of architect William Robertson in 1890/92. Some time after the reunification of the presbyterian churches in 1929, Stromness, in common with many other places, found itself with a surfeit of church buildings and solved the problem by turning the Free Church into the town hall and the parish church into a community centre.

Church Road is one of the most aptly named streets in Stromness. On the left, in this view from Victoria Street, is the Free Church and on the right St Mary's Episcopal Church, while crowning the scene is the old Parish Church, which dates from 1814.

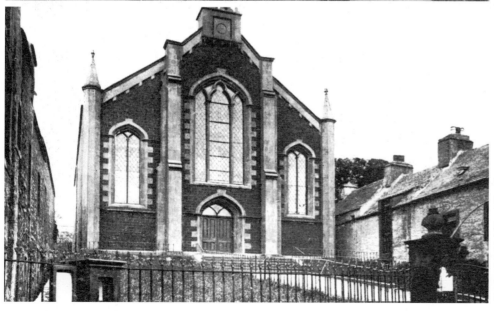

The United Presbyterian Church in Victoria Street was built in the 1860s to the designs of Richard Spence. It became the United Free Church when the U. P. and Free Churches amalgamated in 1900 and, after reuniting with the Church of Scotland, became the Parish Church.

The upper and lower left of these pictures show Victoria Street in the early 1950s and about 1910. The lower right picture shows Dundas Street looking toward Graham Place, named after Alexander Graham, a Stromness merchant who challenged the right of Royal Burghs in Scotland to levy taxes on other places that did not enjoy the rights and privileges of Royal Burghs. This ancient right was at odds with a provision in the Act of Union allowing free trade, and as shipping in and out of Stromness grew, so did the taxes paid to Kirkwall. This caused resentment among the merchants and, as their leader, Alexander Graham started a legal challenge in 1743 that dragged on for fifteen years before it was upheld in the House of Lords. Graham thus broke the stranglehold on foreign trade enjoyed by the Royal Burghs, not just between Kirkwall and Stromness, but throughout Scotland. It was a hugely important victory, but it bankrupted Graham whose name deserves to be more widely known. At least in Stromness part of the street has been named after him and a fountain at the pier head dedicated to his memory.

Despite its many changes of name the street barely changes character. It is narrow and with an irregular building frontage on either side it meanders in a general north/south line, but is rarely straight for any distance. Paved, with a cobbled centre to allow horses hooves to get a better grip, it is delightful. At one time parts of it were so narrow that alterations had to be made to allow the passage of wheeled vehicles, although the speed of modern traffic and the size of some vehicles can make this an uncomfortable experience for pedestrians. The upper pictures show the same section of Dundas Street at the start and middle of the twentieth century, the lower picture, also from the mid twentieth century, shows the junction with Hellihole Road. The street name also changes here from Dundas Street to Alfred Street.

Numerous closes branch off the street, like ribs off a spine. Short, more direct, closes run down to the shoreline, but those that take the town up to the high ground to the west, often go by a more labyrinthine route. Meandering around the contours and rising variously by steps, stairs, and cobbled slopes they give the town a highly distinctive character. This close adjacent to Rae's stationery shop, with its luxuriant plant life, was used by a postcard publisher as an example of a 'picturesque close'. Since then the foliage has disappeared and the enticing view up the hill has been obscured by a, not so picturesque, corrugated iron building.

Millar's Close off John Street takes its name from the Millar family house seen here facing camera. The sandstone pediment above the door is carved with the family coats of arms, the date 1716 and the inscription 'God's Providence Is My Inheritance'.

This view from the tower of the former Free Church looks north-east across the town towards the South Pier, with the Stromness Hotel prominent on the left. In the foreground the walls and buildings show the way the town spread uphill with narrow, walled plots between the closes.

The more haphazard development of the upper part of town is evident in this view also taken from the Free Church tower. The rear portion of the parish church, formerly the United Free Church, is on the left. The vacant ground between the older town in the foreground and the large villas on the high ground has since been filled with municipal and modern housing.

In June 1924 the steamer *Cape Wrath* arrived from Montrose loaded with 300 tons of building materials, including 60,000 bricks. The following morning the shipping company laid on two motor lorries and over twenty carts, and thirteen hours later the cargo had been unloaded and taken to Springfield Crescent where the first twelve municipal houses in Stromness were to be built. The scheme, designed by T. S. Peace, had been delayed, so ceremonial was dispensed with, so that the contractors could press ahead and complete the first houses by the end of the year.

At its most southerly end the street is called Ness Road and is seen here looking north toward the town. The cannon in the foreground is reputed to have come from an American privateer, the *Liberty*, captured in 1813. It was apparently fired to alert the townspeople to the arrival of a ship requiring men or provisions. A bench here gives visitors, tired after their walk from one end of the town to the other, a place to rest and enjoy the fine view of the harbour.

The houses along Ness Road also enjoy fine views of the harbour. The large building with the double gable, tucked in behind the last house on the left, was built in 1892 as the shore station for the Sule Skerry lighthouse, providing accommodation for the keepers and their families.

The Northern Lighthouse Board serviced its most northerly buoys and lighthouses from a base and pier off Alfred Street in Stromness. Three lighthouse tenders, all named *Pole Star*, operated at various times from the base. The first, launched in 1892, was replaced in 1930 and she in turn was superseded by another new ship in 1961. The second *Pole Star* is seen here passing Graemsay with the looming bulk of Hoy behind. On the right is the lighthouse known as Hoy Low which, along with Hoy High lighthouse, was erected in 1851 to guard the entrance to Scapa Flow and Stromness. Both were located on Graemsay, not Hoy, but their names did accurately reflect their size: Hoy High was 110 feet tall and Hoy Low 40 feet.

Looking across Hoy Sound to Ward Hill and St John's Head, a farmer is seen here using an ox to plough a field to the west of Stromness. This use of oxen to drive ploughs or pull carts, was a popular theme of early photographers who used it to show how primitive life was for rural Orcadians. In doing so they missed the point, that cloven hoofed beasts often coped better with soft, wet ground than horses and that the farmers were just being practical. The farmer in the lower picture has hedged his bets and yoked a horse and a cow to the plough, allying equine strength with bovine traction.

Attempts to reform farming practices began in the second half of the eighteenth century, but had little impact before the people's attention was diverted by war with Napoleon, and the economic depression that followed. Through the early decades of the nineteenth century therefore land use remained wasteful and inefficient. Numerous tiny plots were divided in such a way as to give everyone access to ground where they could grow crops, while their animals roamed at will on common land. Change began in the 1830s as landowners began to break up the small haphazard units to create larger holdings. Consequently agriculture has become the dominant feature of the Orkney countryside, often surprising visitors who expect to see a landscape scattered with smallholdings as in other crofting counties.

In the early days of subsistence farming, oats and bere (a form of barley) were grown in rotation with no variation. Some flax and a few potatoes were also grown. After the land reforms, oats, turnips or potatoes were rotated with grasses, for either hay or pasture. Gradually through the first half of the twentieth century grasses became more important as beef cattle production gained in importance, although oats continued to account for more than a quarter of productive land. The huge influx of service personnel during the Second World War created a need for milk and an increase in dairy cattle to provide it. The Royal Navy's departure left a glut of milk which was absorbed into butter and cheese production, but beef cattle, especially Aberdeen Angus, grew in importance and the land became predominantly green pasture. In the upper picture stooks of corn are being collected from a field, while the impressive stackyard below is thought to have won its builder first prize in a competition in 1929.

Egg production was, for a time, one of the most successful aspects of Orkney farming. What started out as a useful way of providing food for the family grew through the nineteenth century into a major export. As the price of oats fell, small farmers found it more profitable to feed the grain to hens, further increasing egg production. By the early 1950s millions were being processed through Orkney Egg Producers which had been set up in the former Ayre Mills at Kirkwall, but then disaster struck. A severe storm in January 1952 destroyed thousands of the flimsy hen houses and over 80,000 hens were simply blown away. There was a partial recovery, but the distance from markets and rise of battery egg production on the British mainland soon rendered the trade uneconomic and scenes like this faded into the past.

Potatoes became an important crop after their introduction in the eighteenth century, although lifting them, as this picture from Orphir shows, was an arduous task. Men turned the ground with large pronged forks while women and children had the back-breaking job of picking up the spuds. Agricultural reform, from which Orkney ultimately prospered, had its down side as many people working small patches of land were pushed off. In some places there were echoes of the brutal clearances across the Pentland Firth in Sutherland, but generally Orkney seems to have managed the change better than most. Many of the crofters or farm workers, known as oncas or bowmen, remained tied to a large farm or estate. They received payment in kind and cash, but were obliged to labour for their superior and only when their allotted tasks were completed, were they able to tend their own plots.

Some of the improving tenants started with small farms and graduated to larger holdings as their fortunes improved. Their houses reflected their relative wealth compared to those of people on marginal land. One such dwelling, at West Brough, Sanday, was built in the mid nineteenth century by Jerome and Walter Dennison who were tenants on Colonel Balfour's land. They also enclosed much of the farm with stone dykes. The Dennisons operated the system of keeping smallholders and labourers on their land in order to ensure that certain jobs like harvesting, thatching, threshing, breaking ground, sowing, gathering seaweed, weeding thistles and cutting peats were carried out.

The contrast between the houses of the well-off tenant farmer and those in less favoured circumstances was stark. Most obviously the ground-hugging buildings seen here, built low to deflect stormy weather, simply look less confident than the Dennison's two-storied house. This unidentified group of structures may have been more than a simple croft: there are outhouses and the building with the flagstone roof appears older than the main cottage, with chimneys, that has been tacked on to it at right angles. It all suggests a degree of evolution, but not wealth.

Having fought in the military campaigns against Napoleon, an Irish soldier named Phinn is reputed to have arrived in Orkney about 1820 and, as Irish ex-soldiers do, opened a pub. Finstown, the third largest community on the islands, is thought to have been named after him. This early twentieth century picture of the village was taken from a spot just to the east of where Phinn's pub was located, on the site of the modern Pomona Inn. The name Pomona was popularly applied to the Orkney mainland in the nineteenth century although it had no historical basis. It has stuck as the name for a variety of catering establishments.

The Firth Parish Church is on the left of this view of Finstown looking west along the Kirkwall to Stromness road. It was built as an United Free Church in 1902, but has since lost the fleche, the little spire, from the centre of the roof. Tucked in beyond the foreground church is a building erected as a Free Church in 1870 and subsequently used as a church hall before being converted into apartments.

The hamlet of Stennes, on the road between Kirkwall and Stromness, has seen a few changes since the mid 1930s when this picture was taken. Mr Linklater's shop on the extreme left has been replaced by another, set back from the road, which also appears to have succumbed to the march of time. The gap beyond the two storey house on the left has been filled by a garage and filling station, and the road surface of packed earth and stones has been covered with tarmac and white lines.

Few hotels reflect the changing face of tourism as well as the Standing Stones Hotel at Stennes. Originally built of timber and known as the Stennes Hotel it was situated beside the Kirkwall to Stromness road, but its position next to Loch Stennes gave it its principal marketing strength as 'Orkney's largest and finest fishing hotel'. Clearly it worked because over the years the hotel was extended a few times taking on an appearance somewhat different to the way it looked in this picture from about 1910. The marketing has changed too: with a World Heritage Site on the doorstep, the archaeology of Neolithic Orkney has supplanted fishing, and proximity to the loch, as the big selling point.

The Stones of Stennes are an impressive sight although sadly they could have been more spectacular. They had stood there from the third millennium B.C. until December 1814 when news reached Kirkwall that the tenant of the estate, Captain MacKay, was breaking them up. His vandalism was stopped, but not before he had toppled two stones, one of which he had broken up. He also destroyed an outlying stone, with a circlular void through it, known as the Stone of Odin. Archaeologists have since established that the fifty foot circle originally consisted of about twelve stones contained within a bank and ditch.

Although only 36 stumps or stones of the original 60 remain, the 340 foot diameter Ring of Brodgar is breathtaking in its scale and setting. Like the Stones of Stennes it dates from the third millennium B.C., but despite its antiquity archaeologists have discovered that it was laid out with mathematical precision, with the stones set six degrees apart in a perfect circle. The rock-cut ditch surrounding the stones would originally have been thirty feet wide and ten feet deep, a truly heroic undertaking for its time.

Storms come and go across Orkney like part of scenery, but in 1850 one of them not only altered the familiar shoreline of the Bay of Skaill, but added a fascinating new find to a landscape already rich in antiquities. What the wind and waves had exposed was a group of previously unknown stone structures and ancient refuse heaps. Subsequent excavation revealed them to be part of a settlement site dating from about 3100 B.C. to 2500 B.C. The principal investigations took place in the 1920s and detailed work on the midden heaps was done in the 1970s. Known as Skara Brae, this little Neolithic village has become the jewel in Orkney's crown as one of the most archaeologically exciting parts of the British Isles. The area's World Heritage status was granted in 1999.

Skara Brae is so remarkable it is easy to overlook other structures in the vicinity, most notably Skaill House seen in the background of this picture. Erected early in the seventeenth century for Bishop Graham it is arguably Orkney's finest vernacular mansion house. Originally a two-storeyed house with a courtyard it was extended with a parallel block and subsequent nineteenth and twentieth century additions.

It was in a thick fog, not a violent storm, that the Aberdeen trawler *Ben Namur* ran aground in the Bay of Skaill in October 1920. There was also a heavy swell running when the boat struck the rocks and two men were washed overboard and drowned. The rest of the crew managed to get a line ashore and were saved. The skipper was found to be negligent and lost his licence for nine months. The boat was a write-off.

Field-Marshal
Earl Kitchener.

Hats off to the Flag
we all love and adore,
And give it a mighty
great cheer,
For with gallant Commanders
like this to the fore -
Old England has
nothing to fear.

In his role as Secretary of State for War, Lord Kitchener, decided to do something about what he regarded as Russia's inadequate contribution to the war effort. In June 1916, a few days after the Battle of Jutland, he boarded the cruiser HMS *Hampshire* and set sail through waters that had not been swept for mines. The weather was so bad that the escorting destroyers could not keep up with the larger ship and were ordered back to Scapa Flow. Keeping close to the Birsay shore to gain some protection *Hampshire* hit a mine and sank in thirty fathoms (180 feet) of water. Admiralty secrecy prevented Stromness lifeboat and local rescuers from going to the aid of survivors and all but twelve men were lost. A few months later, a meeting in Kirkwall decided to erect a memorial tower on Marwick Head. Built by contractor William Liddle of Orphir, to the designs of Kirkwall architect J. M. Baikie, it was 48 feet high and 23 feet square. Lord Horne of Stirkoke, Caithness, unveiled it in July 1926.

The Vikings, and before them the Picts, established settlements at Birsay. The eleventh century earl, Thorfinn the Mighty, made it the site for the first cathedral on the islands and it was the centre of religious life until Earl Rognvald built St Magnus Cathedral at Kirkwall. The Bishops of Orkney retained a residence at Birsay until the sixteenth century, vacating it before the Earl's Palace, which dominates the present day village, was erected. In the foreground is another important structure, the bridge over the Barony Burn, part of which may date from the same time as the palace.

Robert Stewart, the Earl of Orkney, built his palace at Birsay in the later sixteenth century; a plan in the Scottish Record Office shows a date of 1574 as a detail of the construction. The earlier Bishop's Palace may have been incorporated into the building which was arranged around a courtyard with the lower walls well fortified. The upper floors were, apparently, richly furnished and decorated with painted ceilings, while outside there was a series of walled gardens.

The little Harray school, on the left of this picture looking north along the main road to Dounby and Birsay, was opened in September 1876 and closed just a few months short of its centenary in February 1976, the children moving to a new school at Dounby. Before school boards were set up under the 1872 Education Act, churches provided education and the Free Church schoolhouse continued to be used until the Harray school was built. The old Free Church and its school sit lower down the slope from St Michael's Church of Scotland which can be seen on the skyline above the board school. After its closure, Harray school became a pottery for the splendidly self-styled 'real Harray Potter'.

The Orkney West Mainland Agricultural Society had been holding an annual ploughing match since 1859 when, in August 1891, they staged the first West Mainland Agricultural Show at Dounby. It has continued as an annual event attracting large numbers of people, as can be seen in this picture of the show from 1922. Despite the dull, showery weather an increased number of entries attended, with the quality, especially amongst the horses, being high. At the close of the show the judges and their friends sat down to a dinner prepared by Mrs Spence of the Smithfield Hotel, the building on the right with its gable facing the camera.

One of many old customs associated with marriage was the wedding walk which had to cross water twice and ward off the 'peedie folk' with loud noises. This walk at Makerhouse, Dounby, was photographed in 1907. The guests will have gathered at the bride's house and then walked in pairs behind a fiddler or piper to the church. Going to church the bride was accompanied by the best man and the groom by the best-maid, but for the return walk the bride and groom walked together. When they reached the house they were met by the oldest and most respected woman in the neighbourhood, known as the 'hansel-wife'.

A number of large mills have been preserved on Orkney, but so too has one small one near Dounby. Known as the Click Mill it was fitted with a tirl, a vertical shaft with the millstone at the top and horizontal paddles at the foot. The whole arrangement rotated when the paddles were lowered into a swiftly flowing burn. Such mills were common on Shetland's hilly landscape, but rare on Orkney. The Click Mill was built about 1832 and will have had only a small number of users, whereas larger mills were built to serve a whole area.

Woodwick House is a couple of miles to the south of Evie. With its crow-stepped gables and tower it has the appearance of an old style laird's house, but was only built around 1912 for the Traill family. It does, however, incorporate some earlier features perhaps retrieved from an earlier house on the site. It was used to provide rest and recuperation for naval personnel during the Second World War and has since become a hotel. Attractive gardens and bluebell woods have replaced the somewhat barren surroundings of this picture apparently taken during construction.

The circular stone towers known as brochs, are unique to Orkney, Shetland, the Western Isles and parts of mainland Scotland. Most were built on coastal sites, which suggests they evolved as a defence against a sea-borne threat. One of the best surviving examples on Orkney is the Broch of Gurness, on an exposed site on Aikerness. It appears to have been robbed of stone, presumably for other building, which has lowered it from a height that can only be guessed at, but what makes it special are the remains of domestic habitation around it. These show evidence of occupation or activity from the Pictish to Viking periods.

The church on Egilsay dedicated to St Magnus probably dates from the 12th century and is thought to have been built on the site of an earlier church where Earl Magnus prayed before his final, fatal meeting with Earl Hakon in 1117. Despite being roofless, the church is substantially intact and although its round tower is lower than it would have been originally, it is a rare survival of a type which once also existed at Deerness and Stenness.

Gairsay was the base of Svein Asliefarson, a twelfth century Viking. He combined working the land with raiding along the coasts of the British Isles, an activity which ceased in 1170 when he was killed at Dublin. His great hall is thought to have been where Langskaill House was built for Sir William Craigie in the mid seventeenth century. Although fortified at the time, and looking somewhat gaunt in this late nineteenth century picture, it was a fine house that was altered a few years later when the east wing, furthest from camera, was restored.

Rousay's hilly and more varied scenery allows it to vie with Westray for the title 'Queen of the North Isles'. The island has also been dubbed 'Egypt of the North' owing to the number of prehistoric tombs found there, but it has another, less welcome, claim to fame, because, more than any other part of Orkney, its people endured the hardship of clearance in the nineteenth century at the hands of repressive landlords. The process started under George William Traill, who ran his estates from Westness, a typical laird's house dating from 1792 situated on the north west side of the island and seen just to the right of centre in this Edwardian picture.

Lt. General Frederick Traill-Burroughs inherited the estates of Rousay and Wyre from George William Traill, his 'honourary uncle', in the late 1840s, but continued with his military career for over twenty years before taking up residence on Rousay. He was a small, bearded, dapper man, known to local people as the 'Little General', but he had a big impact. Westness clearly didn't match his vaunted opinion of himself, because he commissioned the architect David Bryce to design a large new dwelling, Trumland House, on the south coast overlooking Wyre. It was built in 1872/73. And while the Little General was indulging in personal aggrandisement, he was rack-renting his tenants and forcing them off the land.

The activities of the Little General, and those like him in other parts of the country, came under scrutiny in 1883 when a Royal Commission, set up under Lord Napier, began to look into the conditions of crofters and cottars in the Highlands and Islands of Scotland. The resultant Crofters Holdings (Scotland) Acts of 1886 and 1887 gave tenants greater security, but a lot of damage had been done and the landscape significantly altered from what it might have been. Deserted steadings, like this one on Rousay, are not as common on Orkney as elsewhere.

Compared to the other northern islands Rousay is hilly, reaching a peak of 815 feet above sea level at Blotchnie Fiold. Cliffs characterise much of its northern coastline, as this picture looking beyond a croft to Eday shows. The picture also shows that the rock that makes up the island's geology splits easily into the kind of flags that don't blow away in a gale when used as a roof.

Major Thomas Balfour built a house overlooking Elwick Bay on the south west corner of Shapinsay in 1782. In 1846, his grandson, Colonel David Balfour, commissioned the architect David Bryce to enlarge it. He not only did that, but over the next four years created a grand Scots Baronial mansion with a castellated and turreted tower rising above the entrance. The house, formerly known as Cliffdale, was now Balfour Castle. It has also been dubbed 'calendar castle' because it apparently contains 365 windows, 12 exterior doors and 52 rooms! To complete the imposing scene a fortified arched gateway, adorned with the Balfour coat of arms, was built in a commanding position above the harbour.

Balfour village, seen here looking across Elwick Bay with the Point of Dishan on the left, was founded as an estate village in 1785 by Major Balfour. His descendant, Colonel Balfour, also carried out extensive agricultural improvements on Shapinsay. It became one of Orkney's most productive farming areas, famed for the high quality of its cattle.

The lighthouse on Helliar Holm, off the south coast of Shapinsay, was built to assist ships passing through The String, the channel between the island and the mainland. The 43 foot tower and associated buildings were designed by engineer David A. Stevenson and built in 1893. The light was automated in 1967.

Although the Helliar Holm lighthouse was directly opposite the Head of Work it was unable to prevent the River Class destroyer HMS *Itchen* going aground one night in September 1909. Her position would have been badly exposed if the wind had come round to the south east so an anxious navy took off the coal, guns and other movable items to lighten her. The first attempt to get her off failed, but with nature's help in the form of three heavy seas she was refloated. HMS *Itchen* seemed to like hitting bits of Orkney, having broken two propeller blades during an earlier encounter with the skerry in Scapa Bay. Launched in 1903, her eventful life came to end in July 1917 when she was sunk by a U-boat while on convoy duty to the east of the Pentland Firth.

If there is one place that nails the myth that Orkney had little or no fishing industry it is the island of Stronsay and its principal village, Whitehall. With its harbour protected by the island of Papa Stronsay, it provided a safe haven for Dutch fishermen who gathered at the start of the herring season, just as they did at Lerwick in Shetland. They did this for a long time before the great herring boom of the late nineteenth century, when local boats and boats from the east coast of Scotland joined in the free-for-all.

At the start of the boom the principal Scottish boats were known as Fifies or Zulus. The Fifie with a vertical bow, slightly raked stern and wide beam was an excellent sea boat, as was the Zulu with its sharply raked stern which gave it greater speed. The first Zulu was built in 1879 during the Zulu War, hence the name, and for the rest of the nineteenth century these sail-driven boats reigned supreme, unless the winds were light when they could be stuck in harbour, or worse becalmed at sea with a deteriorating catch. The advent of the steam drifter changed all that and by 1910 these boats had largely displaced the sailing craft as this picture of Whitehall Pier shows.

Whitehall village grew up close to where a former laird, Pat Fea, had built his house in the late seventeenth century. The area was known as North Strynzie, but James Fea, Pat's son, changed the name to Whitehall and that stuck when the pier and village were built in the 1820s by Malcolm Laing of Papdale. The main purpose behind the development of Whitehall was to encourage cod fishing, so when the herring boom really kicked off in the late nineteenth century the island already had an indigenous fishing industry, but it was small compared to the number of boats and people that arrived for the herring season.

The season started in late June and continued through to August. At its height curing stations were spread along the sea front as coopers, gutters and packers filled barrels with salted herring for markets in Russia and northern Europe. A fish market erected at the pier head in 1913 gave skippers an incentive to land their catch at Whitehall and it must have seemed as if the bonanza would go on for ever, but the silver darlings were being overfished and after reaching a peak about 1905 the fishery began to decline. It was largely halted during the First World War and never fully recovered afterwards. Attempts to revive it in the 1920s and 1930s only delayed the inevitable and by the outbreak of the Second World War Whitehall's days as a fishing port were over. This picture of the village in the 1930s, and the upper, undated picture convey a sense of the decline.

James Fea did more than just select the name of Whithall, and was also responsible for establishing the kelp industry on Orkney. Kelp is the product left behind after seaweed has been burned, and although the industry became established throughout Orkney, Stronsay, with its three huge bays, was an ideal place to pioneer it. After the seaweed was gathered, here cut with a sickle and carried from the shore in a kishie, it was laid out to dry before being burned in a shallow pan or kiln. When it cooled it formed a solid mass that was shipped to chemical manufacturers, mainly in the north of England, who used it as an alkali in the making of various products.

James Fea started the kelp industry about 1722 and for the next 100 years it provided a good income, although there was some opposition to the creation of this new source of wealth. The fishing and farming industries were deprived of a labour force, because people were diverted into this more lucrative business, often by landowners who set the labour against a crofter's rent. Fishemen also believed that harvesting seaweed for kelp production adversely affected the fish, and farmers, who had long used seaweed as a fertiliser, resented its use for something else. The industry peaked in the 1820s and then started a steady decline although, as these pictures show, seaweed was still being gathered and burned in the early years of the twentieth century.

Peat, the islanders' traditional winter fuel, was cut from moorland banks where the decaying roots of mosses, heather and other plants had built up into a compact mass. The process began with the top surface being stripped off and laid aside where it would regrow. The peat would then be sliced by a bladed implement known as a tusker. Skilled operators could cut and lay the peats aside in a single movement, although here a woman is helping by lifting and laying the slabs of peat. The boys seem content to watch. After the peats had lain for a couple of weeks they were set up in little groups to help them dry and they would be taken off the moor only when much dryer and lighter to carry.

Peat cutting was carried out at the beginning of May. The day started early with the family heading out to the peat bank armed with the tools and sufficient sustenance to last through a long hard day. Breakfast was had after a couple of hours of toil and in the middle of the day the hungry workers sat down on the heather for dinner (lunch). Beer and sandwiches appears to be on the menu for this group, some of whom are also in the upper picture. Their clothes and general appearance suggests they were enjoying a day out cutting peat because they wanted to, rather than because they had to, and indeed, with more coal being imported, peat was becoming less essential in the early twentieth century when this picture was taken.

Sanday (the name means sandy isle) is indeed a low-lying sandy island that was hard for mariners to see in adverse weather or poor visibility and numerous skippers drove their ships onto its shores unaware that they were close to land. In the days of wooden ships this was good news for the locals, because there was no peat on the island and a free delivery of smashed up firewood was very welcome. Fortunately for whoever took this picture, the ship they were on, probably the north islands steamer *Orcadia*, had made safe passage to the island (it looks like an arrival rather than a departure because no-one is waving). The vessel is coming alongside Kettletoft Pier which could be exposed to difficult conditions if the weather was coming from the south or south east.

Kettletoft, the main community on the island, is seen here with *Orcadia* alongside the pier on the left. During the great herring boom it profited briefly from fishing, but never on the scale of Whitehall on Stronsay. For Sanday, agriculture was always the principal activity.

Membership of the United Presbyterian Church on Sanday outgrew the church building and so a new church was built at Roadside to accommodate a congregation of 800. The new building, designed by the architect Samuel Baikie, is seen here under construction in 1881, in a photograph taken by John B. Russell of King Street, Kirkwall. With the Established Church of Scotland, the Free Church and United Presbyterians all having separate places of worship, Sanday was over-supplied with churches when the three disciplines amalgamated in 1929 and this structure, erected with such evident pride, fell into disuse.

The newly established Commissioners of the Northern Lighthouse Board built one of their first four lighthouses on Dennis Head, North Ronaldsay. Completed in 1789, it had the unintended effect of drawing ships to it, to take a bearing, and in doing so they came dangerously close to Sanday which was enough of a hazard without the new lighthouse adding to the dangers. To counteract this a 75 foot tower, designed by Thomas Smith and Robert Stevenson, was erected in 1802 on Start Point and the old beacon on North Ronaldsay was decommissioned. The first revolving light in Scotland was fitted at Start Point in 1806 and the original stone-built tower was replaced in 1870 with the brick one in this picture. This was later painted with dramatic black and white vertical stripes to distinguish it from other lights. It was fully automated in 1962.

Westray, the most westerly of the northern islands, is also the most scenically varied and a claimant to the title 'Queen of the North Isles' for which it competes with Rousay. The principal village, Pierowall, is seen here from the south clinging to the shore of a lovely bay. Unlike more modern villages, like Whitehall, it is an ancient settlement site although most buildings in this early twentieth century picture date from the nineteenth century. The Norsemen recognised the value of the partially enclosed bay as a harbour, and evidence of Viking habitation and burial sites has been discovered. Archaeological excavation has also revealed a prehistoric village, not unlike Skara Brae, on the nearby Links of Notland.

This view of Pierowall appears to have been taken on the same day as the upper picture. It shows the central part of the village with, on the left, the school and baptist church. It dates from 1850 making it a relatively recent addition to the list of Pierowall churches. Earl Rognvald is known to have worshiped in a church here in 1136 before his campaign to avenge the murder of Magnus. That church is long gone, but its successor, the Lady Kirk, remains as a ruin of largely seventeenth century origin, but incorporating fragments of thirteenth century masonry.

Westray School, built in 1875 in the wake of the Education Act of 1872, became one of the few schools in the country to be visited by royalty when Queen Elizabeth and the Duke of Edinburgh were escorted round the building in August 1960 by headmaster Norman Cooper.

The Royal Visit to Orkney created quite a stir. The Queen and Prince Philip arrived at Stromness and after a tour of the mainland left Kirkwall on the Royal Yacht *Britannia* heading for Westray. On arrival, the Duke drove a new school bus a mile to the newly modernised school and after the inspection, drove back. At the pier the Queen was presented with a bag that had been made by a local woman, Mary Kent, using sealskin caught and cured on the island. The Royal couple then left on *Britannia* bound for Aberdeen, and their annual holiday at Balmoral.

Apart from its churches and school, Pierowall's villagers and visitors have been able to use amenities like shops, a post office, heritage and craft centres and even a swimming pool. There is also the Pierowall Hotel, erected early in the nineteenth century and, for long periods, the only hotel on the island. The Bayview Temperance Hotel at Gill Pier, a rival from the early twentieth century, is seen on the right of the lower picture.

Although the harbour was good, it was not deep enough for large vessels and so the island's principal pier was on the northern edge of the bay at Gill, where this group of houses was situated. The pier was also used by fishing boats, but while this industry dwindled elsewhere, it thrived and grew on Westray with a varied fleet of whitefish trawlers and smaller boats geared to crab and lobster fishing. A factory was erected at Gill Pier to process the catches and provide employment. The main inter-island ferry has switched to Rapness in the south, but the boat linking Westray and Papa Westray still uses Gill Pier. The air journey between the two islands is of course famous as the shortest scheduled flight in the world. A flight from Westray ranks high on the list of your scribe's memorable moments. Fog had delayed our chartered Loganair plane and when he arrived, the pilot looked at our gear (we had been filming on the island) and suggested we start to jettison it if it looked as if the plane wouldn't clear the wall at the end of the grass runway. It did, he chuckled and we all breathed again.

Gilbert Balfour was a Fifer on the make, not a pretty sight at the best of times, and 1560, when he acquired Westray through marriage, was not the best of times. He appears to have begun building Noltland Castle immediately and its forbidding appearance suggests he had enemies. It is built on a Z plan and, with over seventy gun holes in the lower walls, it is ideal for defence with firearms. Balfour's tempestuous life ended with his execution in Sweden in 1576, but the castle remained in use for about two hundred years during which time a courtyard and outer buildings were added.

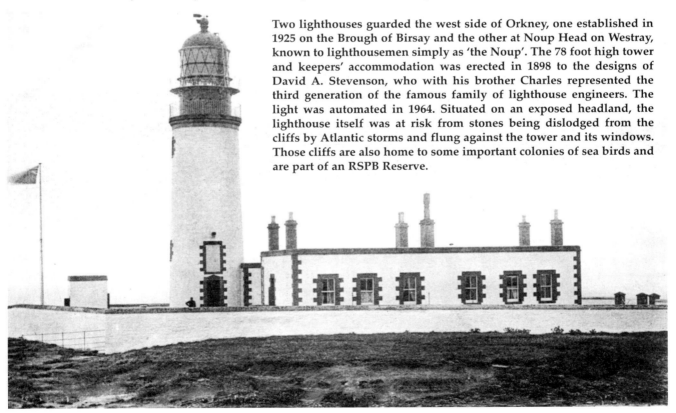

Two lighthouses guarded the west side of Orkney, one established in 1925 on the Brough of Birsay and the other at Noup Head on Westray, known to lighthousemen simply as 'the Noup'. The 78 foot high tower and keepers' accommodation was erected in 1898 to the designs of David A. Stevenson, who with his brother Charles represented the third generation of the famous family of lighthouse engineers. The light was automated in 1964. Situated on an exposed headland, the lighthouse itself was at risk from stones being dislodged from the cliffs by Atlantic storms and flung against the tower and its windows. Those cliffs are also home to some important colonies of sea birds and are part of an RSPB Reserve.

Rapness, at the southern end of Westray, was served by two places of worship, a Church of Scotland parish church and a United Free Church. They existed almost side by side which meant that when the churches united in 1929 the larger of the two, the United Free, became the parish church and the smaller was made into the church hall.

There are a few places called Holland in the Northern Isles. It means high land in Old Norse and because it was the best place for a farm and dwelling it is usually where the largest house in an area was built. Holland, on Papa Westray, came into the hands of Earl Patrick Stewart's chamberlain, Thomas Traill, in 1636, and the family subsequently built a house on the island's prime piece of real estate. Parts of the building may be from the seventeenth century, although the main structure most likely dates from the early nineteenth century.